modern readers · stage 2

The Phoenix

Eduardo Amos
Elisabeth Prescher
Ernesto Pasqualin

Richmond

© EDUARDO AMOS, ELISABETH PRESCHER, ERNESTO PASQUALIN, 2004

Diretoria: *Paul Berry*
Gerência editorial: *Sandra Possas*
Coordenação de revisão: *Estevam Vieira Lédo Jr.*
Coordenação de produção gráfica: *André Monteiro, Maria de Lourdes Rodrigues*
Coordenação de produção industrial: *Wilson Troque*

Projeto editorial: *Véra Regina A. Maselli, Kylie Mackin*

Assistência editorial: *Gabriela Peixoto Vilanova*
Revisão: *Denise Ceron*
Projeto gráfico de miolo e capa: *Ricardo Van Steen Comunicações e Propaganda Ltda./Oliver Fuchs*
Edição de arte: *Christiane Borin*
Ilustrações de miolo e capa: *Félix Reiners*
Diagramação: *EXATA Editoração*
Pré-impressão: *Helio P. de Souza Filho, Marcio H. Kamoto*
Impressão e acabamento: *Forma Certa Gráfica Digital*
Lote: 783422
Cód.: 12037266

Dados Internacionais de Catalogação na Publicação (CIP)
(Câmara Brasileira do Livro, SP, Brasil)

Amos, Eduardo
 The phoenix / Eduardo Amos, Elisabeth Prescher, Ernesto Pasqualin; [ilustrações Félix Reiners]. —
São Paulo : Moderna, 2003. — [Modern readers ; stage 2]

 1. Inglês (Ensino fundamental) I. Prescher, Elisabeth. II. Pasqualin, Ernesto. III. Reiners, Félix.
IV. Título. V. Série.

03-3366   CDD-372.652

Índices para catálogo sistemático:
1. Inglês : Ensino fundamental   372.652

ISBN 85-16-03726-6

Reprodução proibida. Art. 184 do Código Penal e Lei 9.610 de 19 de fevereiro de 1998.

Todos os direitos reservados.

SANTILLANA EDUCAÇÃO LTDA.
Rua Padre Adelino, 758, 3º andar — Belenzinho
São Paulo — SP — Brasil — CEP 03303-904
www.richmond.com.br
2023
Impresso no Brasil

Ahmed is from Vichy, France. He's the son of a Moroccan businessman and a French school teacher. His father travels a lot. Now that Ahmed's mother is dead, the boy and his father live in Figuig, Morocco.

Ahmed is at home, in his father's office. It is the end of the school year. The boy is looking down at the school report on his father's desk. He is worried... very worried.

Just then, Ahmed's father enters the office.

"So, here you are," he says. He looks down at the big, red letters, F-A-I-L-E-D, on the report. Then, he looks at Ahmed. And he is angry... very angry.

"Father, I can study hard next year..." Ahmed says nervously.

"I don't want your promises," his father shouts. "I'm tired of your promises."

Ahmed's father looks at his son and sees a model plane in his hands.

"You and your model planes!" He walks over to the boy and grabs the model plane.

"But, father, I love them."

"I don't care! I don't want any model planes here! Do you hear me? No more model planes! Next year, I'm going to send you to Fez to study. You are going to stay with your grandmother."

"But, father..." says Ahmed, trying to speak.

"That's enough! My decision is final."

4

Some weeks later, the small airport in Figuig is crowded. The school vacations are over now. Many people are going back home. Ahmed is at the airport too. A new school year is beginning and he's going to live and study in Fez.

Figuig is a small town in Morocco, in the Sahara Desert. It is about 500 kilometers from Fez, and the flight is not very long — only an hour and a half over the desert and the Atlas Mountains.

Now it's time for Ahmed to board the plane. It is a small plane. It can only carry fifteen passengers.

Five minutes after takeoff, the plane is flying over the desert. Ahmed is in a window seat. He is looking out. The view of the desert is beautiful.

Soon, Ahmed takes a piece of paper out of his backpack. He starts to draw airplanes. First, he draws a single-engine airplane and then a twin-engine one. He draws small planes and big ones.

A man is sitting next to him. He looks at the drawings.

"You like planes, don't you?" the man asks Ahmed.

"Yes, I love them."

"I'm Neil Harris," the man says. "What's your name?"

"Ahmed Ali Kaam," the boy says. "Do you like planes, too?"

"Very much. I'm an engineer and I work on airplanes."

"Do you build them, Mr Harris?" Ahmed asks.

"No, I just fix them."

"I like to build model planes, and I like to draw. Look!" Ahmed shows his drawings to Mr Harris.

"Well, I like your drawings," Mr Harris says. "You have a good imagination."

"One day I'm going to draw a real airplane, Mr Harris."

Half an hour later, the captain makes an announcement:

"Ladies and gentlemen, this is the captain. There is a big sand storm ahead of us. I'm going to try to fly around it."

The plane flies to the right, then to the left, then it goes up. But small airplanes can't fly very high. Soon the plane is in the middle of the sand storm. Everything inside the plane shakes. The wind is very strong. Many passengers are frightened now. Two women are crying and an old man is praying. Ahmed is worried.

"Are we going to crash, Mr Harris?" Ahmed asks.

"Of course not," Mr Harris says calmly. "These storms are common in the desert. Everything is OK." Harris tries to comfort Ahmed but he is worried too.

"Mr Harris," Ahmed shouts. We are going down! We are going to crash!"

Ahmed is right. The wind is stronger now. The plane continues to shake.

"We are losing altitude," the captain announces. "Prepare for a crash landing."

Ahmed looks out of the window. He sees the desert very close to the airplane. Then, the airplane hits the ground suddenly. People scream and shout in panic. The airplane jerks to the right, then to the left. Another big jerk and the engines stop. For two or three seconds, there is complete silence. All they can hear is the wind blowing outside.

"Are you OK?" Mr Harris asks Ahmed.

The boy is still in shock. He can't hear Mr Harris.

"Ahmed! Are you OK?" Mr Harris insists.

"I think so," the boy answers softly.

A man opens the door and people rush out of the plane.

"Please, calm down, everybody!" the captain shouts. "There's no risk of fire. Stay near the plane."

But the passengers are too frightened. They try to walk away from the plane, but they can't go far. The wind is too strong and they can't open their eyes.

A few minutes later, the storm is over. The sky is clear now and a hot breeze is blowing. Slowly, the passengers start to walk back. They gather under the wings of the plane. Some passengers are hurt, but not seriously.

After checking the airplane, the captain says in a grave voice, "I have bad news. One of the engines and the wheels of the airplane are broken. Our radio is out of order too. We can't take off and we can't radio the airport."

"We only have enough water for four days, and some sandwiches, biscuits and fruit," says the copilot checking inside the plane.

Just then, Mr Harris has an idea. "Let's write SOS on the sand! We can use colorful clothes to make it. Maybe another airplane will see us and send help."

After a day in the desert, there is no sign or sound of a plane.

"What are we going to do now, captain?" Mr Harris asks.

"Well, we are off route because of the storm. Probably 100 kilometers."

"So, that's why we can't see any planes," says Mr Harris. "What can we do?"

"Nothing," says the copilot. "The only thing we can do is wait for them to look for us."

"Are the passengers inside the plane?" the captain asks.

"Yes. They are sleeping," says the copilot.

"Desert nights are very cold," the captain adds. "This boy is freezing. Let's get inside too and try to get some sleep."

DAY TWO

The next morning the sun rises beautifully in the east. Some of the passengers are getting impatient.

"There is no sign or sound of airplanes in this area," a man says.

"So what do we do now? Wait to die here in the middle of the desert?" a woman asks.

"I'm going to find help," a man says.

"How are you going to do that?" the captain asks.

"I'm going to walk until I find a village or a caravan."

"Are you crazy?" says the captain angrily. "If you walk away from here, you'll die. There's nothing in the desert!"

Ahmed is sitting on the sand next to the airplane. He is holding a piece of paper and a pencil. He is drawing.

Under the hot sun of the desert, the argument is still going on when Ahmed shouts.

"I have an idea."

He holds up his drawing. His idea is to use the good engine of the airplane and make a 'flying wing'.

"The captain can fly it out of here. He can get help," Ahmed says.

"This boy is out of his mind!" a man shouts.

"Yes, he is crazy! His idea doesn't make sense!" says a woman.

"Stop dreaming, little boy! We are in serious trouble," a man says angrily.

"But I am serious," says Ahmed.

"The boy is right," Mr Harris says. "His idea is logical… and possible. I'm an aeronautical engineer and I think the boy's idea is good. We can try it."

The captain looks at the drawing. "I think it can work," he says. "And a flying wing is not difficult to fly."

"I am a mechanic," one of the passengers says. "I want to help. I have my tool case with me."

"I can help, too," another man says. "So, let's build a flying wing and get out of here!" shouts Mr Harris.

DAY THREE

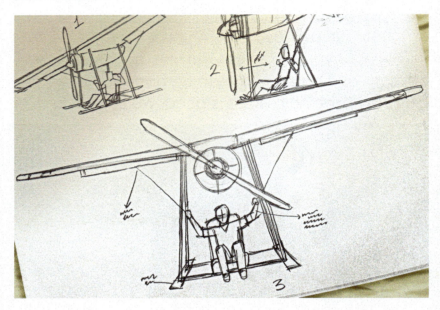

This is Ahmed's drawing.

It is very hot in the desert during the day. It is impossible to work outside the plane.

"We have a problem," says the captain. The wheels of our plane are broken. How is the flying wing going to take off?"

16

"Maybe we can make a pair of skis," the mechanic suggests.

During the night, they work outside.

The passengers don't have much water and food, but they have hope in their hearts.

17

DAY FOUR

It is the end of the fourth day. They only have enough food for one more night and very little water. But the flying wing is ready.

DAY FIVE

At five o'clock in the morning, the passengers pull the flying wing up to the top of a dune. When the sun finally rises, the flying wing is ready to go. "Wait, please wait!" shouts one of the women.

She runs back to the airplane and takes a can of black grease. Then she walks up to the flying wing and writes "P-H-O-E-N-I-X" along it in black letters.

"Now the flying wing is ready. You can go, captain," she says.

"Turn on the engine, now!" Mr Harris shouts.

Ahmed looks anxiously at the flying wing. All the other passengers and the copilot cross their fingers.

The captain starts the engine. There is a loud roar and the propeller slowly starts to turn. The captain accelerates and the flying wing slides down the dune.

In a few seconds, the Phoenix is up in the air. It climbs higher and higher. Then it disappears into the horizon.

"Mrs Clusot," says Ahmed, calling the woman. "What does Phoenix mean?"

"You see, I'm a History teacher. I'm going to tell you all about it," Mrs Clusot answers. "Let's sit under the wing."

By afternoon, there's no more water. Everybody is worried but nobody says a word. All they can hear is the hot desert breeze blowing against the airplane.

But suddenly, they hear a very soft sound in the distance. They turn and look. There are two spots on the horizon. The spots come closer and closer and the noise of the engines gets louder. Soon, two rescue planes are flying over them. They jump, shout and hug Ahmed.

"I don't believe it! We are safe!" cries one of the passengers hugging Ahmed.
"Thanks to you, Ahmed," another man shouts.
"And thanks to the Phoenix!" Ahmed says and smiles at Mrs Clusot.

KEY WORDS

The meaning of each word corresponds to its use in the context of the story (see page number,00)

ahead (8) em frente
along (19) ao longo
argument (14) discussão
backpack (6) mochila
blow, blowing (9) ventar
board (5) embarcar
breeze (11) brisa
broken (11) quebrado
build (7) construir
businessman (3) executivo
carry (5) carregar
clear (11) limpo
crash (9) bater
crash landing (9) pouso de emergência
crowded (5) cheio
cry, crying (8) chorar
dead (3) morto
desk (3) mesa
down (3) para baixo
draw (6) desenhar
drawing (6) desenho
dream, dreaming (15) sonhar
engine (11) motor
everything (9) tudo
failed (4) reprovado
fire (10) fogo
fix (7) consertar
flight (5) vôo
flying wing (14) asa voadora

freezing (12) sentindo muito frio
gather (11) reunir-se
go back, going back (5) voltar
grab, grabs (4) agarrar
grease (18) graxa
ground (9) chão
hard (4) muito
hit, hits (9) bater
hold, holding (13) segurar
hope (17) esperança
hug (20) abraçar
hurt (11) machucado
jerk (9) solavanco
lose, losing (9) perder
model plane (4) aeromodelo
office (3) escritório
outside (9) fora
pray, praying (8) rezar
propeller (19) hélice
ready (18) pronto
rescue plane (20) avião de resgate
rise, rises (13) levantar
risk (10) perigo
rush out (10) sair correndo
sand storm (8) tempestade de areia
school report (3) boletim escolar
scream (9) gritar

21

send (4) enviar
shake, shakes (8) balançar
shout, shouts (4) gritar
sign (12) sinal
single-engine (6) monomotor
ski, skis (17) esqui/s
slide down (19) escorregar
softly (10) suavemente
sound (12) som
spot (20) ponto
tired (4) cansado
tool case (15) caixa de ferramentas
travel, travels (3) viajar
trouble (15) encrenca
try, trying (4) tentar
turn on (19) ligar
twin-engine (6) bimotor
vacations (5) férias

wheel (11) roda
work (15) funcionar
worried (3) preocupado

Expressions

cross (their) fingers (19) cruzaram seus dedos
It doesn't make sense (14) não faz sentido
I don't care (4) Eu não ligo
in shock (10) em choque
it's time (5) está na hora
just then (4) naquele momento
Of course not! (9) É claro que não!
off route (12) fora da rota
out of his mind (14) fora de si
out of order (11) quebrado
That's enough (4) Chega!

ACTIVITIES

Before Reading

1. Look at the title of the book. What do you know about "The Phoenix"?

While Reading

Pages 3 – 5

2. True or False.

    a. (   ) Ahmed lives in Morocco.
    b. (   ) Ahmed is happy because school is over.
    c. (   ) Ahmed's school report is good.
    d. (   ) Ahmed is going to study in another city next year.
    e. (   ) Ahmed is going to fly over the Sahara Desert.
    f. (   ) The plane is very big.

Pages 6 – 9

3. These sentences are wrong. Correct them.

    a. Ahmed draws the desert.
    b. Mr Harris builds planes.
    c. Mr Harris thinks they are going to crash.

Pages 10 – 12

4. Read and answer:

    a. Who is in shock?
    b. Who tells everyone to calm down?
    c. Who checks inside the plane?
    d. Who suggests they write SOS in the sand?

Pages 13 – 15

5. Why is the captain angry?

6. What is Ahmed's idea?

Pages 16 – 17

7. There are some problems with Ahmed's plan. What are the solutions? Complete the table.

PROBLEM	SOLUTION
1. It's too hot to work outside during the day.	
2. They don't have any wheels	

Pages 18 – 20

8. Ahmed asks Mrs Clusot, "What does Phoenix mean?" What is she going to tell him?

After Reading (Optional Activities)

9. In the story, Ahmed lives with his father. His mother is dead. Is it difficult to live without a mother or a father? Discuss.

10. Ahmed is from France, but he lives in Morocco. Is it difficult to live in a foreign country? Discuss.

11. Find out all you can about Morocco, the country where Ahmed lives. Include:
- people   - food
- geography   - history

12. Ahmed's father sends Ahmed away because he "failed" at school. What do you think about his decision?